A Love Story to Remember

Daughter of a Sharecropper

By

Bessie Townsend

Copyright ©2019 Bessie Townsend

All rights reserved. No part of this publication may be reproduced, distributed, or transmitted in any form or by any means, including photocopying, recording, or other electronic or mechanical methods, without the prior written permission of the publisher, except in the case of brief quotations embodied in critical reviews and certain other noncommercial uses permitted by copyright law.

ISBN-13: 978-1-951300-83-8

Liberation's Publishing LLC
West Point, Mississippi
www.liberationspublishing.com

A Love Story to Remember
Daughter of a Sharecropper

by

Bessie Townsend

Table of Contents

Making A Way 7

Change 17

Becoming A Young Lady 25

Married 37

Temptation 47

A New World 53

Dedication 70

Bessie Townsend

Making A Way

Having thirteen children is inconceivable in today's time when children are considered a burden, but when I was a child, children were a blessing and the more a family had the better off they were at providing for themselves. I grew up the daughter of a sharecropper, the oldest daughter of thirteen children consisting of eight boys and five girls. As the Psalmist wrote, "Lo, children are a heritage of the Lord: and the fruit of the womb is his reward. As arrows are in the hand of a mighty man; so are children of the youth. Happy is the man that hath his quiver full of them: they shall not be ashamed, but they shall speak with the enemies in the gate." (Psalm 127:3-5 KJV)

My mom, dad and us thirteen children lived in a shack located on the plantation we sharecropped. There were many families that lived there, and most of them were fairly large like ours. Sharecropping was a way to provide, but it did not bring the freedom it promised. We were free by law but not by deeds. Let me explain.

Our family didn't own the land we worked. We didn't even own the house we lived in. The plantation owner owned everything, and we were considered tenants, renters. The payment for our rent was most of our crops and our labor. We would chop and pick cotton in his field to stay on his land and in his house.

Our springtime's were spent chopping cotton. My family was responsible for sixty acres. Those sixty acres were divided into four fields. Anyone older than six years old was required to go to the cotton fields. This included my mother. When I was six, I had to babysit the younger children, and we only went to school when it rained.

Chopping was what seemed like a never-ending cycle. Most of the time when we would finish chopping one field the first field would have already grown back, and we would start all over again. There were even times when we had finished chopping our crops only to be hired out to other plantations for four dollars a day to help with their chopping.

Sometimes when we were in the field, the boss would have the crops sprayed with pesticides by a small airplane. He would never tell us when he was going to spray, and we would get sprayed with pesticide. I remember us running trying to get away from the spray as the pilot would laugh at us as we ran. I often think that this is what caused the cancer in my family. My Mother and Father would die from cancer. Two of my brothers would go on to have cancer as well as myself. I think that airplane had everything to do with it. I am so thankful that God took care of us.

My oldest brothers worked the hardest; they had to work all of the fields, corn, hay, and cotton. Now me, being the oldest of the girls was taught how to cook at a very early age by my mother. We didn't have a clock, television, or electricity. We had a wooden stove and heater.

That's what I cooked on.

My mother was a very strong woman, and my father was a great provider. They worked very hard to provide for us thirteen children. My dad worked at the gin where the cotton would go after harvesting. He raised hogs, and had a beautiful garden filled with almost every vegetable that you could think of. My dad was also a great hunter, and he taught his sons how to hunt too. I never remembered going hungry or going without.

In hindsight, I don't know how we made it through those days except by the Grace of God along with my mother's great faith. She would teach us bible class every Friday night. Bible class would help us to read. That helped us a little, but we always fell behind all the other children in school. They were fortunate enough to go to school every day.

Those children that had the luxury of going to school every day had parents that owned their own land and fields. They only had to work after school. As I said earlier, we were only allowed to go to school when it rained. If we didn't work, we would be put off of the plantation, and that was our home. There was nowhere else to go. Because of this, not being able to go to school daily, we were labeled the "Brand" children by our classmates and teacher. In spite of it we learned as much as we could.

My Brothers would get up early in the morning to get the mules ready for plowing the field. During planting time, the boss didn't have a tractor. They used manual plows hooked up to the mules. Every family was assigned two mules. Our mules were named Kate and Ellen. They would plow every day, all day; sixty acres of land, forty to fifty rows to plant cotton on. They had to hold the plows in the ground while the mule pulled. I don't know how we made it, except by the grace of God.

With sharecropping my parents didn't get paid weekly. They were paid once year, but there was a grocery store on the plantation that allowed each family to have a line of credit until the end of the year. The end of the year is what was called "Settle Up" time. That being said, my parents borrowed money from the plantation owner throughout the year to buy clothes and other things our family needed.

I also remember that a seed check was given each time a bale of cotton was picked. We picked about three bales of cotton a week, and the check for the seed in the bale would be two to three dollars. Each bale had to weigh at least thirteen to fourteen hundred pounds.

I remember it didn't take a lot of money back then. You could take three dollars and buy groceries for a week. If you wanted a snack, a quarter would get you a drink, a package of donuts, a pack of crackers, a can of Viennas and four cookies.

Neighbors took care of one another. Having a baby meant a mom would be in bed for at least six weeks. If she didn't have any daughters old enough to help, a neighbor's daughter would come over and cook and clean until those six weeks were up. We had good Christian neighbors that helped. Everyone shared food and when a hog was killed that meat was shared with other neighbors. Every neighbor owned hog for meat. Women felt comfortable borrowing stuff like meal and sugar from one another. They would pay you back once they came into their own. No one would talk about each other because that was the way it was.

I remember, there was a woman who made clothes for everyone for a small fee. She would measure you, and they clothes would be a perfect fit. I remember is when I was staying at home keeping my sister and brother, my mom would get the food ready to cook for the next day. She would tell me what time to put it on the stove. Since we did not have a clock, she would put a stick on the ground, and when the shadow was in a certain place, I would have to put the pot on the stove on. When the shadow moved to another place, I knew to take the pot off of the stove. We had different ways of doing things back then.

My father taught us to predict the weather by the different kinds of clouds. I still do it today. My daddy could shoot a perfect shot with his gun. If he had six bullets; he would kill six rabbits. He did not believe in wasting ammo. He was so creative; he made a weapon called a tap stick. He would get a long stick and attach a large bolt to it. He would throw it at rabbits and kill them. He killed many rabbits that way and he taught the boys how to hunt that way too. He couldn't always afford bullets or to buy the boys a gun.

Ball games were our favorite pastime. Our neighborhood had many teams that played against other communities. We had a great team and we won most of the games. There were a lot of house parties. When someone had a birthday, the whole neighborhood would come as well as some kids from other areas. Someone would spin records and we would eat chips, drink Kool-Aid and put a blue light on the porch. We would dance in the yard for hours.

Bessie Townsend

Change

When my brothers got old enough, they wanted to find jobs. They wanted to leave the field, but my daddy didn't want them to go. Daddy was afraid we would be put off of the plantation. My brothers went anyway. It ended up being okay because there were still enough of us left to chop and pick cotton.

Shortly after that some of my other brothers wanted a job, so they left. One after another they left until there were only five of us. The boss man started to complain, and we knew that he was going to ask us to leave soon.

God had a plan though. My older brothers gave my father enough money to buy an acre of land from one of my father's cousins that lived fifteen miles away. Not only did they buy land, one of my brothers bought a mobile home for the acre of land. Our family couldn't stay on the boss's land any longer. Soon after that, my father and mother put in for an FHA home and were approved. They had to do all of this in secrecy. They didn't want the boss to see them leaving, because they were afraid of what he might do.

It felt good to purchase our own home. Usually when my daddy or one of the other families wanted to get a car the boss would sign for it, but the family would have to make the payments. When the house was built it was just momma and daddy signing. The house was a three-bedroom house, and there were twelve children still at home.

My parents had to put two full sized beds in each room and a sleeper couch in the living room. Five girls slept in one room and five boys slept in the other room and two kids slept in the living room on the sofa sleeper. Mom and Dad had their own room. It was very crowded, but it felt good because we were in our own house. We were especially glad we didn't have to go to the fields anymore. If we wanted to, we could chop or go to school full time.

When we moved my Daddy got a job too. He and my brothers all worked at a meat plant. We still went to the same church. In those days the preacher would take turns eating at each member home. My Mother was a very good cook. Everything came out of the garden that was in our yard. Us kids didn't like when it was our turn to feed the pastor. The reason being we could not eat until after the Preacher and some of the Deacons ate. They would take their time talking and laugh while we are waiting for them to leave.

Mother would cook a lot of good food. We didn't have running water or air in the house. So, one of us had to get a piece of cardboard and fan while the guest ate to keep the flies from landing on the food. When one got tired another one of us would take over. I couldn't understand why the Preacher would bring his family and some of the Deacons with him to help eat up our food. There was always enough left, but still.

Daddy would never eat with the Preacher and Deacons. I guess because he rarely went to church and didn't want the Preacher and the Deacons to preach to him about not going to church.

Before we moved to our knew home, we carried water from a pump that was a half mile away because we didn't have running water in the house. We washed in tubs before we owned a washing machine. Water was so far away but the pools where the boss's cattle drank from were close. We carried water from the pool to wash and sometimes bathe in. Mom would build a fire in the backyard to boil the water in. She used a big black pot to sterilize the water.

Since we didn't have much money to buy soap, my Mom and other women in the community would make lye soap to bathe with. They also made meal out of corn with a grinder. Butter was made with a churn and lard from the hog fat. I don't know how everything kept so well in those days. Meat from the hogs was kept in a room dressed in salt for an entire month. A man would come once a week with ice. My parents bought it and it kept too.

I know today it had to be God keeping and providing for us. We didn't have lots of clothes. I was blessed to be the oldest girl I got new things that was passed down to my other sisters. They would be glad to get them, especially bras. We wore our clothes until they tore apart. My Brother would get a pair of long johns once a year and by the time it was warm enough to take them off the bottom was already tearing out.

As far as the girls no one owned their own underwear we all shared them. We would get two pairs of shoes a year, one for school and one for church. Sometimes the shoes would run over. So, at night we would put the bedpost on the side that was run over so it would be straightened out the next day.

Flour and meal came in these pretty printed cloth sacks. My Mother would buy flour and meal in 20 to 40-pound bags. The big cans that the lard came in she used to store the flour and meal.

We would use the sacks and make dresses out of them

We had one church that everyone on the plantation went to. I still attend the same church today. In those times, all the children had to go to church. No one stayed at home. All the women went too, but not all the men just a few of them. The men just sat under a tree at church selling snow cones, talking, or some of them would be drinking. My Father made sure that we went. Other people's Fathers made them go too. I don't know why the fathers felt like it was ok for them not to attend church.

Our church was a little wooden building. It had oil lights, a wood heater, and cardboard or paper fans. The church was about a mile from our homes. On Sundays the road would be full of people walking to and from church. It was fun back then. Everyone seemed to care about each other. People would sing those old hymns. The older mothers and Deacons would sing and pray. The Holy Ghost was in the place. There was lots of shouting.

We would have revival prayer service for a whole weekday and night. Then the next week there would be preaching, day and night. We had a bench called the mourning bench. By the age of twelve if you were not saved you would sit on that bench until you felt the Holy Ghost and accept Christ and confess that Jesus died and rose on the morning of the third day.

Living on the plantation we made our own toys because we did not have money to buy them. Toys were bought once a year and that was at Christmas time. You either got a doll or a tea set. The boys got a toy truck or cap pistols along with apples and oranges. We were very excited about Christmas. Mom would start cooking for Christmas a week early. She'd make four to five cakes, lots of pies, and we either would have a hen or goose dressing. To prepare the goose momma would put it in a pen by itself and feed it corn for a whole week to clean it out. The cakes and pies stayed fresh too. I know it was God, because food spoils now if you keep it out past three days. Mother didn't have a fridge.

We would have greens, beans, potato salad, and corn. We didn't eat like that until the end of the year. I never knew what my parents went through to feed thirteen children, but my mother prayed all the time.

Momma taught us how to pray. Our prayer as children was "Now I lay me down to sleep I pray the Lord my soul to keep." She had so much faith. She talks to the Lord every day. Sometimes she would be crying and talking to the Lord. I didn't understand why she cried, but I knew her prayers worked.

Becoming A Young Lady

Being the oldest girl among my mother's children, was hard. I was the first for everything. I had to endure being a teenager with some very strict parents. I don't know what my Mom might've went through to be so hard on us. I do know when she was a teen, she was well protected.

She would tell us if we got pregnant, she would shoot us, but she never really explained the birds and the bees. It was Just don't let little boys mess with you and that one day I was going to have a period. That being said I was scared, because we believed her about shooting us, even though She never told us how we would get pregnant, but she did say if we miss our period we were with a baby.

I got my period and didn't tell a soul. I didn't tell mom, and I already knew what to do. We made our own pads out of old clothes and burned them afterward. One month, I don't know whether it was stress or what, but I missed my period. I had never been with a boy, but I miss my period. I was so scared. I started praying to the Lord. I didn't tell anyone. My sisters were younger than me; they couldn't help me. So, I pretended to have my period.

I thought that I was chosen to be like the Virgin Mary. When I think about it now, I find it so funny, but the next month it came back on. My boyfriend had kissed me, and I thought that was why I was pregnant.

When I was thirteen a neighbor's boys, Sam, asked my Mom could he come and court me. He didn't ask me or show interest in me before this. It was like it was not up to me to say yes or no. I didn't like that he didn't give me a choice. Anyway, mom told him I wasn't old enough, and when I turned fourteen, he could court me. The nerve of him. He even asked my mom, "You're going to let me be the first to come see her right?" Mom agreed and he waited a year.

During the wait, I had a boy or two that liked me in school. But one day after I had turned fourteen, I met the love of my life, Johnny. He was three grades ahead of me. We would talk often at school. Meanwhile the boy that my Mom promised me too was waiting his chance.

My birthday was coming up and Sam, the promised boy, didn't know anything about it. Johnny my newfound love, wanted to come see me. I asked mom and she said yes. I think she had forgotten all about her promise to Sam. Johnny came to see me and Sam found out about it. He was upset and came to my house.

"You told me that I would be the first to date her," he reminded my mom. Mom told him, "You can still come see her." No one asking me anything as usual. I told my mom; I didn't like Sam that way. She said you don't have to marry him just be nice to him. He had nice parents. They had cows, and my Mom wanted her girls to marry someone that had something. Johnny 's family didn't have much but that's who I liked.

Johnny had dreams and he was ambitious.

Our Mom was strong, and we had to do what she said, even if we didn't want to. In those days a boy could only come to see you twice a week. So, Sam came to see me on Tuesdays and Sundays and Johnny came to see me on Wednesdays and Saturdays. I was very cold to Sam. I didn't even let him hold my hand or kiss me. It seemed like that made him like me even more. I thought if I wasn't nice to him, he would leave.

Johnny, I liked him very much. I was ok as long as they didn't meet up on the same night. The only reason I saw Sam was because of my Mom. She wouldn't let me tell him not to come to see me. One Sunday evening Johnny decided to come and see me without telling me. Sam was already at my house. He showed up and I was so scared. Johnny demanded I tell Sam to leave and Sam wanted me to tell Johnny to leave. I personally wanted to tell Sam to leave but I was afraid of my Mom.

So, I didn't tell anyone anything. I am sitting there not knowing what to do. So, Johnny got mad, rushed off, got in his car, and sped off. He ran his car into the ditch. I thought that he was hurt, Sam was happy. Me and four of my brothers rushed down to the ditch to see what happened. Johnny was just sitting there dumbfounded. My brothers picked up the car and sat it on the road, and before we knew it, he sped off kicking up rocks everywhere. I didn't hear from him the rest of the summer.

I didn't have a phone or an address to write him. I was so sad. My mother felt so sorry for me. She said if he cares for you, he will be back for you. Sam kept coming over. Sam and his family went to the same church as our family. His family was hoping one day that we would marry, but I didn't like him that way. In his head I guess he felt that since Johnny was gone, he had a better chance with me. That wasn't the case all I could think of was Johnny.

I was angry with Sam for staying around. He

told his Uncle that we were getting married. I got really upset and at that point I didn't care what my mother said. I told Sam not to come back again. He was very hurt. I know that he was very hurt because the next Sunday his big sister, who was grown, pulled me to the side after service and asked me why I hurt her brother. I was afraid of her but not afraid enough to let Sam back into my life.

I prayed for the lord to help Johnny and me get back together. I had never felt that way about someone even though I was only fourteen. It was a long summer for me. We would hardly ever go to town, but one Saturday my Mom took me downtown with her. Sure enough, we ran into Johnny and he wanted to talk to me and wanted to know why I couldn't make a choice between him and Sam. I explained to him my reason. We made up.

It was Johnny's last year in school we fell in love. He asked me to go to his senior prom with him. My Mother and Father were very strict. I couldn't go to the prom without a chaperone. In fact, everywhere we went together my brother, or my sister would have to go. They were so afraid that I would get pregnant. My brother John went with me. I knew we didn't have much money, but somehow my Mom bought me a pretty dress for the prom. Johnny brought me a pretty corsage.

Arriving at the prom I noticed some of the girls my age was allowed to go to the prom without their brother or sister. I didn't want anyone to know my Mom didn't trust me. So, I ask my brother to stay in the car, and he said ok. I had a good time with Johnny at the prom, but when we got ready to leave, we went outside to find my brother walking around talking to everyone. I was so upset with him. All he could say was I got tired of sitting in the car.

Johnny graduated and went off to college, and later he got drafted into the Army. Before he left though, he asked me to marry him. I said yes. I didn't tell my mom because I was afraid. She had told me before that I was too young to get married, but in that moment, I didn't care because I was in love.

It was a custom that if you were to get pregnant you had to go ahead and marry the father of the child. So, when I finally told my mom about being engaged to Johnny that is the first thing she thought. My mom instantly wanted to know if I was pregnant. I was able to proudly let her know that I wasn't and not only that, but I was still a virgin.

Shortly after that, Johnny began to send me an allotment which was a check. The goal was to begin saving for our wedding. Now keep in mind I was still a senior in high school. During this time Johnny was in boot camp. We would send each other letters back and forth and you could only imagine how much I had missed him. After boot camp Johnny came home and guess what? We still weren't allowed to go out alone. This was insane to me but, trust and believe we found a way to get some alone time without getting caught.

Sadly, Johnny had to leave again. A month has passed now, and I missed my period. This time I was really scared and didn't know what to do. Then another month passed, and I missed it again. It was just my luck that I would get pregnant my first time. I wrote Johnny to tell him about what was going on, and he told me not to worry. He suggested that we'd move our wedding up and that way I didn't have to tell anyone. My mom was very happy about the wedding date being moved up and began to plan things.

I couldn't keep my pregnancy a secret, so I told one of my sisters. She knew that we couldn't tell our mom because it would make it hard on them when they dated. So, days passed, and mom had a beautiful dress made for me. We had a chandelier in the living room, my mom used it to have me some beautiful earrings made. My sister in law who was also one of my best friends was my maid of honor and my sister Stine was a flower girl. We didn't have all those fancy decorations and expensive food that you have today, but we did the best we could with what we had.

A local church was having a group singing, so we were able to get married there in between songs. Rev. L was Johnny's cousin so he agreed to marry us. Nervously I headed to the church and I suddenly remembered I left the marriage license. Johnny began to think I stood him up because it took me so long to get back. I made it back and this was Reverend L's first wedding so all three of us were up there nervous.

We got married and went back to my Mom's house. When it was time to go, I wanted to ask my Mom if I could go with Johnny. We ended up having a two-day honeymoon at a motel and then afterwards stayed a week at Johnny's Grandmother's house. I had never met her. When I did, I could really tell how old she was and how direct she was. She asked Johnny where he had got this "little girl" from. Johnny just said that I was older than I look. I was 18 by that time.

Johnny was stationed to Texas at Fort Hood. I went back to school. He wanted me to finish my last year. I went for quite a while, until I started to miss him just as much as he started to miss me. We ended up deciding that I'd quit school and get my GED in Texas.

Bessie Townsend

Married

I had never been out of Mississippi or flown on an airplane before. He couldn't take leave to come and get me, so I had to fly over to Texas alone. My Mom was afraid of me flying and my Daddy didn't have much to say, except he loved us very much. He'd tell us how much he loved us when he was drunk. I had to leave my friends from school and they really didn't want me to go. I only had one year left to go, and there were a lot of memories made in my high school years. But the time had come for me to live with my husband.

It was hard for me to leave my family at home. My Mom and all of my sisters cried. As I got onto the plane, to my surprise, I wasn't afraid. I changed planes two times. The first flight landed in Dallas, Texas. Then I got onto a small 8 passenger airplane that took me to Killeen, Texas. From there, I took a taxi to Fort Hood. Johnny had duty as a guardsman at the gate and saw me coming, so they let him off work to spend time with me. We went to an apartment that he was sharing with Al Green's brother, who happened to be in the same company as Johnny. To my surprise, Al Green's brother would be leaving in a month, and Johnny and I would take over the rent.

It was like the honeymoon I never had. The first time truly being away from home. I was very shy, we were alone, without any friends from back home. My Husband had a couple of friends, but they were people from his company. I cooked and cleaned. We didn't have a car, but we lived in town and I would walk most places. Eventually Johnny bought a car because we needed one,

Johnny was the perfect husband, and when I got closer to my due date, he was so nervous. If I hurt just a little bit, he wanted to take me to go to the hospital. That would end up happening two to three times a week.

I asked Johnny if I could go home to have our

baby. I wanted to be near my mother anyway since this was my first child. He said yes, and I honestly think to this day that he was relieved. I think I was driving him crazy. He ended up driving me home, and I was so excited. I had missed my family. Johnny stayed for about a week before he had to head back to Texas. It was very sad to see him have to go back.

My Mom had a phone, but it was a party line. I know some of you might not know what that is. It worked like this. A party line was an open phone line that two, three or more homes had access to at the same time. Only one person could talk at a time, but everyone with a receiver could hear that person's entire conversation. The thing is only one could talk at a time. If you were on the phone, no one else could use it. You would have to wait for them to hang up. Everybody was so bad about listening in and eavesdropping. Luckily, you could hear when someone else picked up in the middle of the conversation.

We had a neighbor, so bad, who would

eavesdrop on everyone's conversations. My Mom and another person decided to play a trick on her. They were going to make her give herself away by talking about her over the phone. Sure, enough she started listening in while they were talking about her. At some point she couldn't take it no more and busted in and started cussing them out. They even told her that they knew it was her eavesdropping on everybody. That sort of stopped her from doing it.

Johnny would call me every other day or whenever he was able to get the line to open. My Mom and sisters were so sweet waiting on me. A couple weeks passed, and my pain started. My brother took me to the hospital that night, and my sister went with me. They called Johnny's company and he said he'd be there as soon as he could. He wanted to be there when the baby came. By two o'clock in the morning my water finally broke. I was having a seven-pound baby boy. that was the worst pain I had ever felt.

Johnny didn't make it in time, but Johnny said

he felt like he knew that I was having the baby. He tried calling my Mom but of course, someone else was on the phone. He ended up calling the operator. He told her that he needed to get through because his wife was having a baby. The operator broke in on the line and told the person to get off due to an emergency. Johnny was then able to call my Mom. She told him that it was a baby boy.

While Johnny was talking to my Mom the operator was listening and had congratulated us for the successful delivery. He was able to come home a few days later to meet his son. He was so proud, and so we named the baby boy Nicholas. Nicholas wasn't able to come home for over two weeks because he had jaundice. I didn't understand what jaundice was, but either way it cleared up. We brought him to my mother's house.

My Mom was old fashioned. Once you had a baby, you weren't allowed to go nowhere for at least six weeks. It was frowned upon to go in the kitchen, or get in a tub, or wash your hair. Johnny didn't believe in this. He wanted his family to see his child. It was just two weeks and my Mom had a fit when Johnny said that he was going to take us to his Grandma's house.

I didn't want to go, but I had to do what Johnny wanted so we went against my Mom's wishes. When we made it to his Grandma's house she fussed too. After two more days Johnny went back to Texas. About a year later, Johnny's time in the Army was coming to an end. He said let us have another baby while we could afford it, before he got out of the service.

I stayed at home for about a month with our new baby. I didn't have a baby bed, so my Mom pulled one of the drawers out of her dresser and made me a crib for my baby. During that time, Johnny found another place for us. It was a bigger place, but he had a friend that wanted to bring his wife and child out there. He let them stay with him until they could find a place of their own. They were from Mississippi too. Then he decided to come and get me and the baby. My Mom and sisters had grown attached to Nick. It was hard again to leave. Johnny came and got us, and we drove back to Texas.

The couple that stayed with us were nice but more mature. They had a baby boy as well. Johnny said that his friend's wife's name was Debbi and that his friend's name was L. I had never cooked on a gas stove before and didn't know how it worked. Every morning Debbie would come in and light the stove for me as well as cook for L. Then I'd cook for Johnny

We got along for a while but after a long while Debbie was doing things that I didn't like. I didn't like the fact she washed her baby in the dish sink and would wash out dirty diapers in the sink too. I wasn't used to that, I felt like that was just nasty. I never said anything, I'd just clean it out with Purex. Soon, it was time for them to leave and I was so glad.

I watched Debbie light the stove several times,

so I thought that I knew how to do it. One morning after they had gone, I got up while Johnny was still in bed. I turned the gas on to make some breakfast. I didn't see any matches, so I went to go find some while the gas was still on. I finally find some matches and walked back into the kitchen to strike the match. The entire kitchen lit up in flames and the blaze jumped all the way into the bedroom where Johnny was.

He jumped up out of bed and ran into the kitchen where stood holding the match in my hand, frozen. My face and arms were burning as he kept asking me what happened. I explained to him what I did. He said oh no, you can't leave the gas on and go looking for matches like that. He told me that I could've blown us off this block.

I was shaking and went to the bathroom to wash and cool off. I washed my face and my eyebrows and eyelashes fell off. I touch my hair and most of it fell off. I looked a mess. We were about to go to Mississippi that weekend, but I was ashamed to go home until my hair grew back.

After that Johnny wouldn't let me light the stove again.

While we were still at Harper Heights, I got pregnant with my second child. So, again I decided to go home and be with my mother. I would end up having another son, Michael. Johnny came to Mississippi to meet his second son. After that visit Johnny would have to go back to Texas and in two months, he came back to take us with him. When we arrived, we had a new home. Johnny rented us a mobile home because it was cheaper.

Bessie Townsend

Temptation

We had to downgrade a little because now we had two kids. The neighborhood we lived in was not the best, some would say it was unsafe. Johnny made new friends and one I remember was Greg who also lived there in the community. Greg was engaged to a girl in Mississippi. News travels fast. Greg was not being faithful and when the news traveled to his mistress that he had a bride to be in Mississippi, the mistress told the bride to be that she was pregnant. This hurt the bride to be and she left him.

I didn't really like Greg. When he returned, he had married his mistress. He brought her over. I was a little shy, but she was very outspoken. Not only that, she was flirtatious too. She would flirt with Johnny , but I wasn't threatened so I ignored it. I would have to show her around and take her places because she didn't drive. Soon, I started to feel comfortable around her and they would come over and eat dinner with us often.

She had a son who was older than my second son so we would go out to the park a lot. Soon we were all making new friends. Johnny and Greg would go out to the training field for sometimes thirty days or more, so Carol and I would spend a lot of time together.

There were other soldiers in the park, who would come out looking for women who did not have a husband. These soldiers were from other companies, so they knew that some of our husbands had gone to field. I didn't want to be unfaithful to Johnny so I wouldn't talk to any of the men. However, Carol loved the attention. She began messing around with one of them and even going out to different clubs. I would keep her son while she did whatever she did. She was very spoiled.

She came from money, but for me I was simpler and had more Godly views. Later, Greg would make passes at me at times. I was young, so I would tell Johnny every time. Greg would stop by pretending he was looking for Johnny knowing he had just left Johnny. Soon Greg stopped coming by.

I got bored and wanted to get a job. Keeping the two boys and not having an outlet was stressing me out. So, Johnny said we should take the kids to Mississippi to stay with my mama for a while. We took them home to Mississippi and we went back to Texas. I found a job at the mess hall where the soldiers ate. It was nice and I was able to meet a lot of new people. We took our lunch break outside. There would always be a very handsome man in a beautiful black caddy waiting. He would be there talking to us he was very nice.

I didn't know anything about a pimp at the time or that he was one. He told me that I was pretty and that he liked me. He would tell me how smart I was. Later, he would start coming around during lunch every day to see me. I didn't tell Johnny because I liked him. One day Johnny came to visit me during lunch, and he saw me and the man talking. Johnny asked me what a pimp was, and I didn't know. He said, that's what that man was! As you can imagine that was my last day at the job. It was a little hard to believe, but Johnny was more mature than me, so I believed him.

I wanted to go get my kids back. so, we took a trip to Mississippi. My sister had fallen in love with my boys and didn't want them to leave. My baby didn't want to come to me. I was so hurt. I told Johnny I would never leave them for that long again. When we got ready to leave my sister cried. She had been taking care of them like they were hers. Soon we went back to Texas. Johnny got ordered to go to Germany for three years. I wasn't sure if I wanted to go. So, we took a thirty day leave before we had to go. My mom and dad didn't want us to go.

We went and got our passports. Johnny was also able to put in for family housing so we would be prepared when we got to Germany. When the month was up, we flew out. This was the longest flight I had ever taken. I thought we would never ever get there but we did. We had to fly over water for about eight hours. We landed in Frankfurt Germany. They put us up in a hotel for the night. We were so turned around due to the time zone difference. That was only the beginning of our mix ups.

Bessie Townsend

A New World

We were supposed to be staying at Kisner base. However, were currently in Wurzburg Germany. We had to make a call and ended up taking a taxi. When we arrived at the base, we found out they hadn't saved us any space in the quarters. They ended up putting us up in a quest house, but it was more like a hotel room. There were many other people living there too. It was a very old time looking and the rooms didn't have bathrooms. The bathrooms were down the hall, and you had to share it with the others. We were provided a meal ticket, but we had to go across the road to get it. It was such an inconvenience.

There were advantages too. Everyone we met were very nice and helpful. Being in the military was like being in another world. Back home people were so racist. Here, it seemed like the military was color blind. I guess it's because they had each other's back during battle. A great example of this is when Johnny got assigned to his company.

One of the guys he met told him, he and his wife would be glad to let us stay with them until we got our own place. So shortly after, we moved in with them. They didn't tell us they had a dog. I did not like dogs at all. They treated the dog like it was one of their children. The thing was, they didn't even have kids. I was brought up thinking that dogs were nasty. Their dog was too friendly. I think he knew I didn't like him. He would always come around me and sit by me. See the thing was I was not afraid; I just couldn't stand him.

He was a German Shepard, and he would shed so much hair! The hair would be all over the house. No matter where you sit. when you got up you would have hair all over you. Johnny would laugh at me because he knew how I felt. I told him we need to find something quick. I don't know how much more of the dog I can take so he found a place in the Germany Village. There were no houses alongside the road like we have here. All the houses were together in the valley. They had Valleys everywhere. The landscape was so beautiful. There was a strip of brown and a strip of green soil that I thought was so pretty. You couldn't see any of the animals, they were all below ground.

We ended up renting from the nice German family on the bottom floor and we lived above them in a nice apartment. We did not have a car and as soon as we moved Johnny's company had a training field trip for thirty days. Johnny's commander had his wife check on me and the boys while they were on the field to take me shopping for food and If I need to go anywhere. She was black and a very nice person, but her husband was a major and mine was a sergeant.

The army wives couldn't associate with lower ranking soldier wives. However, she would still check on us. They also had taxis which I could use to go places. Johnny was gone for a week and I had two little babies. One was 14 months and the other 9 months. On top of that I was in a very strange place where I was the only one speaking

English.

I started to get so lonely, no phone, no tv or nothing. They had a phone booth down the street, but I didn't know who to call. We had German money, but I didn't know the value of it. So, I asked the Lord to send Johnny back home. I was close to the Lord. I had a lot of faith in God. When I was in Texas I had been going to a church where they believed in fasting and praying. So, I said I will fast and pray. For that whole week I prayed for Johnny to come home on Friday. I would pray every day, drink nothing but water, and one snack a day. I believe God was going to answer my prayer, so I fixed a good meal for Johnny at half past three in the afternoon. I began to set the table and pray.

Then there was a knock at the door. Praise God it was Johnny I was so happy. We greeted each other with a hug and a kiss. He saw the kids and greeted the kids and kissed them also. Johnny looked over at the fully set table and asked, who told you that I was coming home. I said nobody because we didn't even have phones. He asked me how I knew to cook. I told him that I had asked God to send him home, and I fasted and prayed. He did not want to believe me. So, I asked him what happen that you were able to come home?

He drove a tank. He told me the tank broke down and they couldn't fix it. So, his commander said that he was going to let the ones who didn't have anything to do, go home. God is so good you just have to trust him. So, if you ever need anything from the lord. Live the best you can, ask God for it, and have faith that He will do it. I never doubted him, and I acted on faith by cooking for him.

So, Johnny was home for a while we would hear cows, goats, and rooster crowing at night but when we went outside, we wouldn't see any animals or outside. So, we couldn't help but wonder where all the animal noises were coming from. So, one day we were walking in the village we noticed that some of the people were bringing up their animals from underground. We learned later, that's what they did during war times to keep their animals safe from bombings. This is a tradition that they have kept and still use today.

It was a nice neighborhood, there was a little German boy who would come up and do little chores for me like take out the trash and I didn't know the value of money yet. It was a much different than what I was used to. The money was in coins and paper deusk mark $5.00 would be on the coin and 10.00 would be on another coin, but to me it just looked like fifty cents. Little did I know, I was giving the little boy 5.00 every day that he came by.

He never missed a day, he made sure he was there to get my money. Johnny was home one day, and the little boy had come up. As I was reaching to give this young man another coin, Johnny said wait! That's five dollars no wonder he comes here every day. After that, I got a book and began to learn about the currency in Germany. The next time the little boy came by, I gave him fifty cents and I never saw him again.

When we would walk in the village people would look at us strange because we were black. They were amused by our bodies. We were told that the women wouldn't talk to black men but that ended up not being true because a lot of black men had German wives. Soon we had to move again. There were a lot of other military families. I lived in a two-storage apartment again. This time we lived on the top floor.

The couple downstairs was named Ed and Cheryl. Ed was in the company with Johnny. they had a little girl named Jessica who was about three years old. Ed was green, he loved his family so much, but Cheryl was wild and very pretty. The rumor was she had been with every guy in Ed's company. We became friends and kept each other's kids. Then if we needed to go somewhere, they had a car and she knew her way around the town. She used to always wear these little hot pants and I didn't like her coming up to our place showing off her body around Johnny.

I knew she did it on purpose. I knew Johnny

was a man and was going to be checking her out. So, I told her not to come to my house without having on some decent clothes. She respected what I said, so we would ride with her to shop and even go to the movies sometimes. Then it would come time for Johnny and Ed to go to the field again.

Now Cheryl had a friend that would come over and she would ask me to keep Jessica. I didn't like it. So, she would say he has a friend if you want to meet him. I said no ma'am! Then one day we took the kids to a game and food place. Her friend was there with his friend, she introduced us, we talked, I told him I was married, and I don't mess around and he said I'm married too. He went on to say that his family was in the states and he just like to have some fun. I had to let him know that I valued my marriage even if he didn't value his. You can only imagine what happened next, a few nights later Cheryl invited me downstairs to hang out for a little. To my surprise, her friend and his friend were sitting in her living room. I became very uncomfortable, but I didn't leave right away.

We ended up sharing a couple of glasses of wine as a group and soon the friend tried to hit on me and that's when I needed to leave. I announced that I was leaving, and he asked could he walk me up. I told him no, but he insisted, so I allowed him. When I got to my door, he tried to kiss me, but I said NO. I did this in such a way he knew I was serious. I went inside and he left. Then there was a loud knock at the door. I would not get up because I was not letting him in. The knocking continued and got even louder. So, I got up and looked through the peephole and it was Johnny

My heart started to beat really fast. I thank God to this day for the decision I made that day. There's no telling what would have happened if I had let the other man in. I didn't tell Johnny about what had happened that night. If your heart is in the right place, God will protect you. That same night, Cheryl got caught up. They weren't able to work things out. They ended up getting a divorce. Ed was devastated, I had never seen a man cry that much and that hard ever before. He loved his daughter so much, but that wasn't enough to keep them together. That was the last we ever heard of them.

We finally were able to get government housing. We moved into this nice community called Marshall Heights. It was like a breath of fresh air. We were able to meet so many new people. All military families of course. I hadn't been to church since we left Texas and that was something I truly missed. So, when I found out that there was a chapel, you could imagine how excited I was to attend. Being from the south, I was used to the old fashion way of church where there was a lot of singing, praying, shouting and preaching.

I knew that the Chapel may be different, but I really didn't know what to expect. Our first Sunday in the new community came around. I got up early that morning and got ready for church.

When I arrived, I was completely overdressed. When the service began, we sang a song out of a hymn book. After that, the chapelman read a scripture from the bible and said a prayer. Now, I was sitting there getting ready to hear a good old-fashioned word but when I looked up, we were getting dismissed. I didn't know what to think. Needless to say, I didn't go back, I just continued reading my bible and praying at home.

Soon after, I made some friends who invited me to their church. However, this was a different type of church, something called a sanctified church. They believed in God, but they just did things in a different way. So, I went with them and there was a lot of dancing. There was also lots of prayer and there would be preaching. This was more of what I was looking for, so I attended there for a while. Soon I would make another friend named Pam. Pam and I had a lot in common and our friendship began to grow.

One day we were talking about me wanting a job, and she volunteered to keep our kids while I worked. I found a job at a Mercedes Benz plant where they make the seats for the cars. There were some other Americans working there also, but mostly German women. There was one German woman by the name of Karmen, she would translate for us so we could understand what the boss was saying.

My friend Lee who I met while working there was really nice and helpful, however, behind every word she said was a curse word. I ended up working for about a year. My husband didn't really want me to work. So, whatever I made was for me to use however I wanted to. This was great because the Army would pay for all the essentials. So, we were able to save a lot of money. I always wanted to make my own money.

Some of the women there had really nice china sets, German woodwork and crystal. I've always admired it, so I wanted to have some of my own to take home. There were so many beautiful things, so I used that money to buy things like that. Everything was going good until one night while we were sleeping, I woke up and I felt so sad, and alone like nobody cared for me. I've felt that way before and when I did something bad usually happened. I could not go back to sleep for nothing. So, I began to pray and asking God to protect everyone we knew and loved.

After I prayed, I began to smell smoke. I woke up Johnny to see if he could smell it too. So, he went to all of the room in the house and saw nothing. Then he opened the front door. We lived on the 4th floor with nothing but stairs to use to get down. When he opened the door, all he saw was smoke. He quickly closed the door putting wet towels in the door to keep the smoke out. Panicking we looked out the window and saw everyone outside calling and shouting for us. They began to put mattresses on the ground asking us to jump and they would catch us. Johnny said NO just as the Army fire truck pulled up to get us. When they extended the ladder, it wasn't long enough to reach us. It wasn't long before the German fire department arrived, and they were able to get us out one by one. I thank God for his grace and mercy. He will not let anything slip up on his children.

We were compensated for our loss and had to move into another house. Thank God it was still on the base housing. The army would offer a lot of tours to Paris, Rome, England, Britain, and other places. I wanted to go so Johnny said okay, pick one and we would go. The military would get good discounts on the tour. I want to go to Paris, but a friend told me they got sick when they went. So, I picked Rome. One of the couples we met were going to keep the boys for us while we traveled. The trip was for eight days. I was so excited but when it was time to go, Johnny changed his mind and said he didn't want to leave our boys alone that long with someone who wasn't family. So, he suggested that I still go if I wanted to.

I had my heart set on this trip, so I went anyway. I didn't know anyone else who was going and now that I think about it, I was really brave to make that trip alone. We travelled by bus and I was seated with two female soldiers. Sally and Ann, they were white. We talked about a lot of things and when we would stop, we would eat together. We stopped in Switzerland for lunch there we ate at a ski resort. From there we traveled to Rome. Sally and Ann asked me if I wanted to share a room with them, they had booked a room for three but one of their friends didn't come. So, I agreed and the next day the adventure began.

Oh, what a beautiful place it was. We had a tour guide who took us places and let us know when it was time to move on. We visited the Catacomb where the dead were buried in the walls back in the bible days. It was broken up so you could see inside of the tombs. I felt so moved to know how sacred of a place it was. Then we visited the colosseum and the Roman forum and the Colosseum. It was such an emotional moment for me. This was the place where people were thrown to the lions and the Romans would fight to the death for entertainment. They had some of the most beautiful churches you could ever imagine. There was the St Peter's Basilica, Sistine Chapel, and the St Peter's Church of San Pietro in Vincoli. We even went to the Vatican where we thought we saw the Pope.

It only gets better; we were able to see the Mediterranean Sea in Sicily. It was the most beautiful blue sea and as far as the eyes can see. The last night we were there Sally, Ann and I decided to do something on our own, so we went on a horse and carriage ride through the city. It was like a fairytale, the night lights in Rome were just breathtaking. I had the time of my life. I didn't think that would be possible without Johnny, but I thank God for sending me two angels to be with me on the trip. We made it back. The ladies and I said we would keep in touch with each other. As we got off the bus, I could see Johnny and the boys, and I couldn't be happier. I had missed them so much.

As we approached our last year in Germany, I started getting sick. I was afraid, but I already knew what was wrong. After visiting the doctor, I realized I was right, I was pregnant. At this point, I was ready to go back home. When it was time to go home, I was seven months pregnant. When you're that far along, you aren't allowed to fly but by the grace of God, somehow, I made it on that plane and back to the U.S., where I was able to start a new chapter in my life.

I always remember to thank God for everything he has done for me and is still doing in my life. He kept this little sharecropper's daughter in his loving arms from the beginning to the end. He has shown and given me love all of my life. I am waiting now for all the other wonderful things he has for me to experience in his beautiful world.

Dedication

I dedicate this book in the memory of my late husband Johnny F. Gibson. To my children and to my Bowens Family that went through this journey with me. I would also like to send a special thanks to my now husband John Townsend who kept pushing me to write my story. I can't forget my loving daughter Aaliyah and my other team of helpers Edward Brown, Keoni Gibson and Michael Gibson. To Nicholas and Johnny II, I love and appreciate you too. I can't forget all of my loving sisters and brothers.

George Bowens Jr (Rest in Peace)
William H. Bowens
Roger L. Bowens (Rest in Peace)
Rev. Bobby Bowens
Rev. Joe L. Bowens
Rev. John L. Bowens
Earnestine Bowens Dean
Francis Bowens Deanes
Willie F. Bowens
Christine Bowens Huggins
Janet L. Bowens
Mose Bowens (Rest in Peace)

Last but not least, my parents George and Emma Bowens may they Rest in Peace.

I love you all, and may God continue to bless you.

Bessie Townsend

www.ingramcontent.com/pod-product-compliance
Lightning Source LLC
Chambersburg PA
CBHW020121130526
44591CB00031B/252